SUPER COOL SCIENCE EXPERIMENTS

CHERRY LAKE PRESS
Ann Arbor, Michigan

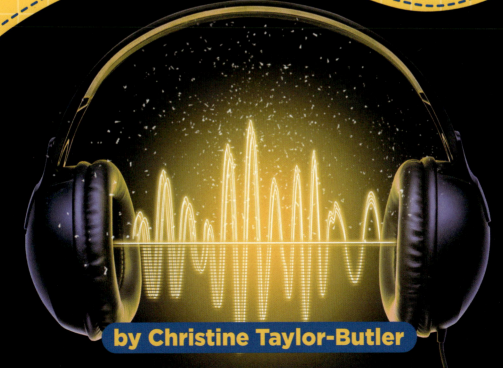

by Christine Taylor-Butler

Published in the United States of America by
Cherry Lake Publishing Group
Ann Arbor, Michigan
www.cherrylakepublishing.com

Reading Adviser: Beth Walker Gambro, MS, Ed., Reading Consultant, Yorkville, IL

Content Editor: Robert Wolffe, EdD,
Professor of Teacher Education, Bradley University, Peoria, Illinois

Book Designer: Ed Morgan of Bowerbird Books

Photo Credits: cover, title page, © Igor Nikushin/Shutterstock; 4, 5, 9, 10, 13, 14, 17, 18, 21, 22, 25, 26, 28, 30, The Design Lab; 5, 6,7, freepik.com; 11, © Profmo/Dreamstime.com; 12, © pakww/Shutterstock; 16, © SvetaZi/Shutterstock; 20, ©My Golden life/Shutterstock; 24, © hodim/Shutterstock; 29, © Andrey Popov/Dreamstime.com

Copyright © 2026 by Cherry Lake Publishing

All rights reserved. No part of this book may be reproduced or utilized in any form or by any means without written permission from the publisher.

Cherry Lake Press is an imprint of Cherry Lake Publishing Group.

Library of Congress Cataloging-in-Publication Data has been filed and is available at catalog.loc.gov

Printed in the United States of America

A Note to Parents and Teachers: Please review the instructions for these experiments before your children do them. Be sure to help them with any experiments you do not think they can safely conduct on their own.

A Note to Kids: Be sure to ask an adult for help with these experiments when you need it. Always put your safety first!

Note from Publisher: Websites change regularly, and their future contents are outside of our control. Supervise children when conducting any recommended online searches for extended learning opportunities.

CONTENTS

Listen Up! 4

Getting Started 5

Experiment 1: 8
Sound and Movement

Experiment 2: 12
Make Waves!

Experiment 3: 16
Rubber Band Music

Experiment 4: 20
Change the Pitch

Experiment 5: 24
Testing the Sound Barrier

Experiment 6: 28
Do It Yourself!

Glossary 30
For More Information 31
Index 32
About the Author 32

Listen UP!

Beep! There goes your alarm. It's time to get ready for school. *Chirp, chirp, chirp!* Birds are singing outside your window. *Ding!* Your dad is making oatmeal in the microwave for breakfast. These are just a few of the sounds you might hear before you've even gotten out of bed. Sounds are everywhere.

Have you ever wondered how people are able to hear? Or how sounds are made in the first place? Want to learn more about sound? In this book, we'll learn how scientists think. We'll do that by experimenting with sound. You can do experiments with things you already have at home. We'll see just how much fun it is to design our own experiments and learn new things about sound!

Getting STARTED

Scientists learn by studying something very carefully. For example, scientists who study sound measure how far sounds travel. They learn how sounds change in the environment. They notice which sounds humans can hear and which ones they cannot. They do experiments to test how sound can be used in daily life.

Good scientists take notes on everything they discover. They record their **observations**. Sometimes those observations lead scientists to ask new questions. With these questions in mind, they design experiments to find the answers.

When scientists design experiments, they often use the scientific method. What is the scientific method? It's a step-by-step process to answer specific questions. The steps don't always follow the same pattern. However, the scientific method often works like this:

STEP ONE: A scientist gathers the facts and makes observations about one particular thing.

STEP TWO: The scientist comes up with a question that is not answered by observations and facts.

STEP THREE: The scientist creates a **hypothesis**. This is a statement about what the scientist thinks might be the answer to the question.

STEP FOUR: The scientist tests the hypothesis by designing an experiment to see whether the hypothesis is correct. Then the scientist carries out the experiment and writes down what happens.

STEP FIVE: The scientist draws a **conclusion** based on the result of the experiment. The conclusion might be that the hypothesis is correct. Sometimes, though, the hypothesis is not correct. In that case, the scientist might develop a new hypothesis and another experiment.

In the following experiments, we'll see the scientific method in action. You'll observe how sound affects the things around it, how sound travels, and how we can influence sounds. You'll develop hypotheses about sound. Next, we'll do actual experiments to see if our hypotheses are correct. By the end of these experiments, we should know something new about sound. Scientists, are you ready? Then let's go!

EXPERIMENT 1

Sound and Movement

First, let's gather some observations. What do you already know about sound? You know that sounds are all around us. Some sounds are very soft. They can be difficult to notice. Other sounds can be loud enough to hurt people's ears. Have you ever been in a car with loud music playing? Some car stereos can produce sounds that are loud enough to rattle the car's windows—or even your body. Have you ever placed your hand against a stereo speaker? The speaker vibrates, or gently shakes, when the bass is turned up.

These observations lead us to a question. Does sound contain an invisible source of energy? Could this energy produce some type of change in an object? Could it cause something to move? Come up with a hypothesis about how sound can act on an object. Here is one possibility: **Sound can be used to make something move.**

Here's what you'll need:

- A roll of clear plastic food wrap
- An empty bowl
- 2 large rubber bands
- A roll of tape
- 1/4 teaspoon of rice
- A metal cookie sheet
- A wooden spoon
- A whistle

· INSTRUCTIONS ·

1. Stretch the plastic wrap over the top of your bowl. Use the rubber bands to hold the wrap tightly against the bowl. If the rubber bands are not large enough to stretch across the rim of the bowl, you can use tape.

2. Sprinkle the rice on top of the wrap.

3. Clap your hands above the bowl. Your hands should be close to the bowl, but not touching it. What happens to the rice?

4. Hold the cookie sheet 1 inch (2.5 centimeters) above the bowl. Bang the cookie sheet with the wooden spoon. What do you observe?

5. Try blowing the whistle near the plastic wrap. What do you observe this time?

6. Stand with your face 2 inches (5.1 cm) above the bowl. Shout as loud as you can. What happens to the rice?

CONCLUSION

What happened to the rice when you made different sounds? Did it move? The sounds you made sent vibrations through the air. These vibrations are sound waves. The sound waves caused the plastic wrap to vibrate. The vibrating plastic made the rice jump. Does this help explain why the rice moved when you made different noises? What conclusion can you make from your experiment? Did you prove your hypothesis?

FACTS!

Ears contain a thin layer of skin called an eardrum. Just like the plastic on the bowl in this experiment, the eardrum vibrates when it is exposed to sound. Tiny hairs behind the eardrum convert these sound vibrations into electrical impulses that the brain can understand. Noises that are too loud can damage these hair cells or the hearing nerve. Try to limit your exposure to really loud sounds!

EXPERIMENT 2

Make Waves

In Experiment #1, we learned that sound causes vibrations. These vibrations contain enough energy to make small objects move. But how does sound travel through the air? Think in terms of direction. Does sound travel in a straight line? In all directions? Think about talking with a friend. Can you only hear your friend if they are talking directly in your ear? Are you able to hear them even if they are behind you, in front of you, or to your side at different angles? Come up with a hypothesis. Here is one option: **Sound travels in a straight line.**

We cannot see sound waves. But we can observe how waves act using water.

Here's what you'll need:

- A cake pan or pie pan
- Water
- A dropper

· INSTRUCTIONS ·

1. Fill the pan halfway with water.

2. Fill the dropper with water.

3. Hold the dropper 3 inches (7.6 cm) above the pan.

4. Squeeze the bulb of the dropper to release a drop of water into the center of the pan. What happens?

5. Wait for the water in the pan to settle. Then release another drop. Record your observations.

CONCLUSION

The pan of water represents air. The drop hitting the water represents the source of a sound. The ripples represent sound waves. In which direction did the waves travel? Was your hypothesis correct?

Vibrations push against the water molecules to make a wave that moves away from an object in all directions. Sound works in a similar way. That is why you can hear a person speak, even if they are facing away from you. The air is also made up of tiny molecules. A sound vibration pushes against the molecules. These molecules bump into other molecules, which bump into more molecules. This forms a wave. As the molecules hit one another, they lose energy. That is why a noise sounds louder if you are standing close to the source and softer if you are standing far away.

FACTS!

In 1886, a German scientist discovered a way to send and receive sound waves through a radio transmitter. Heinrich Hertz designed a wire that would move back and forth in response to sound vibrations. The vibrations could then be measured. Scientists use the term *hertz* (Hz) to describe the **frequency** of a sound wave. A hertz is equal to one wave passing a certain point in one second.

EXPERIMENT 3

Rubber Band Music

You have discovered from Experiment #2 that sound vibrations cause molecules in the air to push against each other in waves. Put your hand in front of your mouth and say, "Ahh!" Say it louder. Now say it softer. Do you feel a vibration on your hand? What question might we ask from this observation? Does it

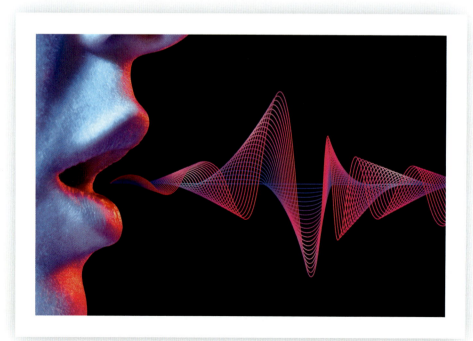

take more effort or energy to make a louder sound than a softer sound? Come up with a hypothesis about energy and sound. Here is one option: **It takes more energy to make a louder sound than a softer sound.**

Here's what you'll need:

- An empty tissue box (one that is longer than it is tall)
- 2 long rubber bands that are the same size and thickness
- 2 thick markers

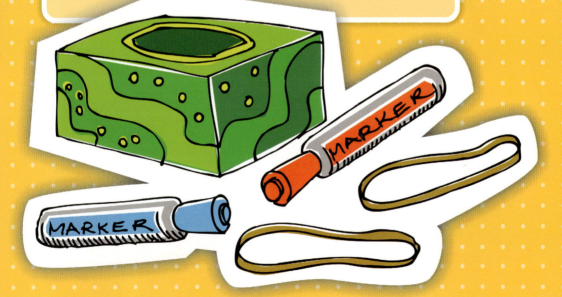

· INSTRUCTIONS ·

1. If there is a thin plastic sheet covering the hole in the tissue box, remove it.

2. Stretch the rubber bands around the length of the tissue box. Space them about 1 inch (2.5 cm) apart. The rubber bands should be stretched across the hole where the tissues come out.

3. Insert the markers underneath the rubber bands so that they are resting on top of the tissue box. Slide one marker to the left. It should reach across the opening of the box but be near the edge of the hole. Move the other marker to the right until it is near the opposite edge of the hole.

4. Use your thumb and index finger to pull one rubber band up 1 inch (2.5 cm). Let go. Observe the rubber band. What sound do you hear?

5. Now do the same with the other rubber band. Is the sound the same or different? Record your observations.

6. Now pull the first rubber band up 2 inches (5.1 cm). Let go. Is the sound louder or softer?

Does the rubber band vibrate longer? Does it vibrate more intensely? Repeat with the other rubber band. Record your observations.

7. Try pulling the first rubber band up 3 inches (7.6 cm). What happens when you release it? How is the sound different from your previous trials? Is it louder? Repeat with the other rubber band.

CONCLUSION

To understand your results, you need to know a little more about sound waves. The height of a sound wave is called the amplitude. Tall sound waves have bigger amplitudes. Sounds with high amplitudes are louder. Sounds with low amplitudes are softer. In this experiment, "bigger" sound waves are those with bigger amplitudes.

Did you notice that the rubber band seemed to vibrate with more energy when it was plucked harder? Was the sound louder when the rubber band had more energy? It takes more energy to produce a loud sound. The energy carried by the sound waves of loud sounds vibrates more air molecules. Was your hypothesis correct?

EXPERIMENT 4

Change the Pitch

We just learned that more energy is needed to make louder sounds. But can we change sounds in other ways? Think about what else you might already know about sound. When you shout or whisper, you change how much air you push past your vocal cords. You also know that vibrations are an important part of sound. What happens when you sing the high and

low notes of a song? Do vibrations have something to do with how high or how low a sound is? A hypothesis could be: **Changing a vibration can make a sound higher or lower.**

Here's what you'll need:

- 4 water glasses that are the same size
- A measuring cup
- Water
- A metal spoon

INSTRUCTIONS

1. Place the glasses on a flat work surface.

2. Use the measuring cup to pour 1/4 cup (59.1 milliliters) of water in the first glass. Pour 1/2 cup (118.3 mL) of water in the second glass. Pour 3/4 cup (177.4 mL) cup of water in the third glass. Pour 1 cup of water in the fourth glass.

3. Gently tap the side of the first glass with the metal spoon. What sound do you hear?

4. Tap the second glass. Is the sound different?

5. Tap the third glass. Pay attention to the sound it makes.

6. Tap the fourth glass. Note the sound produced. Record your observations.

·CONCLUSION·

Which glass makes the highest note? Which makes the lowest note? How do vibrations play a part in the outcome of this experiment?

Hitting the glass with the spoon makes both the glass and the water inside vibrate. The vibrating glass and water transfer their energy to the nearby air and water. The glass with the most water makes a lower sound. The glass with the smallest amount of water makes a higher sound.

When you add water to the glass, it's as if it becomes part of the glass itself. Adding water increases the mass (the amount of physical matter something contains) of the glass. Something with a larger mass creates sounds with lower frequencies. Vibrations with lower frequencies create a lower pitch. Pitch is how high or how low a sound is. Did you prove your hypothesis?

FACTS!

Musicians use similar ideas from this experiment when they play an instrument called a glass harp. They fill many glasses with different amounts of water to match the frequencies of the notes of a musical scale. They run their fingers around the rim of the glasses. This causes the glasses to vibrate and make different sounds. The sounds create a song!

EXPERIMENT 5

Testing the Sound Barrier

You've learned that sound travels through air. What else do we know about sound? We know that sound can change depending on where we are standing. An ambulance siren sounds different when you are outside than it does when you are in a house. How are we able to hear something that is outside when we are inside? Think about it. Could sound have the ability to pass through things besides air? That leads us to our next hypothesis: **Sound waves can pass through a solid object.**

Here's what you'll need:

- Earbuds or headphones
- A phone with an app that plays music
- 2 empty cardboard tubes (paper towel rolls work well)
- A ceramic coffee mug

INSTRUCTIONS

1. Plug in or connect the headphones to the phone. Push the earpieces halfway down into the length of 1 cardboard tube.

2. Turn on the music and put the volume down low.

3. Place the free end of the first tube against one end of the second tube. You should now have one long tube.

4. Put your ear against the free end of the second tube. Can you hear music? Is it loud or soft?

5. Set the second tube aside.

6. Put the free end of the first tube inside the coffee mug. It should touch the inner base of the mug. Then place one end of the second tube against the bottom of the mug on the outside. The base of the mug should now be between the two tubes.

7. Press your ear against the free end of the second tube. What do you hear? Does the sound pass through? Record your observations.

26

CONCLUSION

The surface of the mug is solid. But could you still hear sounds? When sound waves cause a wall to vibrate, the air on the other side of the wall vibrates, too. This is why sound can be heard through walls. How does this concept apply to the setup of this experiment? You could still hear music because the energy of the sound wave passed through the solid mug, from molecule to molecule. The sound waves, however, lost energy as they passed through the mug to the air on the other side. Did you prove your hypothesis?

FACTS!

When sound bounces off an object, it is called an **echo**. Bats, dolphins, and whales use sound waves to locate objects. When the sound wave bounces back, the animal can figure out the distance and location of an object. The navy also uses sound waves to find objects underwater. Special **sonar** equipment is used. Sound travels faster in water than in air. Sonar does not work in space. There are no air molecules to carry the sound waves.

· EXPERIMENT 6 ·

Do It Yourself!

Scientists measure the amount of energy in sound waves in units called **decibels**. We call this measurement of decibels the volume. Scientists experiment with different ways to make it easier for the human ear to hear soft sounds or block out loud ones.

Have you ever noticed that cupping your hand behind your ear can help you hear something? Your hand kind of makes a cone shape. Could holding the smaller end of a cone to your ear make it easier to pick up sounds? How? Is the cone somehow able to catch more sound waves? Does it direct them toward your ear?

To find out, design an experiment. What is your hypothesis? What materials would you need to make a paper cone and run the experiment?

Write out the instructions for your experiment. How many soft sounds can you hear without the cone? How many with the cone? Record your observations.

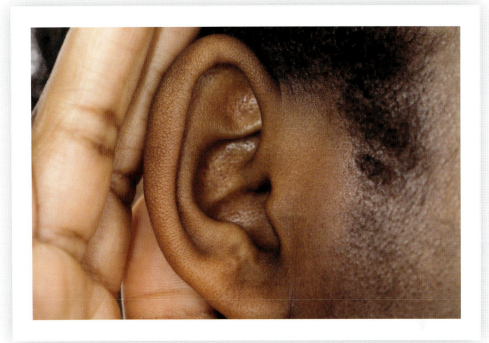

FACTS!

Okay, scientists! Now you know many new things about sound. You learned through your observations and experiments. You also found out that even though you can't see sound waves, their presence is shown in other ways. And you discovered that you, too, can be a scientist and create sound experiments of your own!

Glossary

conclusion (kuhn-KLOO-zhuhn) a final decision, thought, or opinion

decibels (DEH-suh-buhlz) units used to measure the energy in a sound wave and describe how loud a sound is

echo (EH-koh) a sound that bounces off an object and returns to the listener

frequency (FREE-kwuhn-see) the number of sound waves that pass a location in a specific amount of time

hertz (HURTS) a unit used to measure the frequency of the vibrations of sound waves; 1 hertz is 1 sound wave per second

hypothesis (hahy-POTH-uh-sis) a logical guess about what will happen in an experiment

observations (ahb-suhr-VAY-shuhnz) things that are seen or noticed with one's senses

sonar (SOH-nahr) a device that sends sound waves through water and detects when they bounce off of something

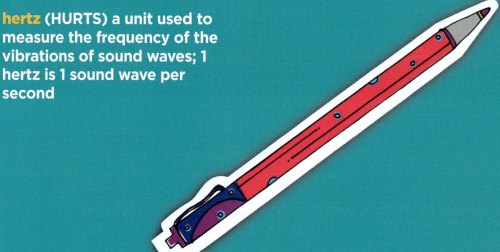

For More Information

BOOKS
Gregory, Josh. *Sound.* A True Book: Physical Science. New York, NY: Children's Press, Scholastic, 2019.

Midthun, Joseph. Samuel Hiti (illustrator). *Sound.* Building Blocks of Physical Science. Chicago: World Book, Ann Arbor, MI: Cherry Lake Publishing, 2022.

Romanyshyn, Romana. Lesiv, Andriy. *Sound: Shhh . . . Bang . . . POP . . . BOOM!* San Francisco, CA: Chronicle Books, 2020.

WEBSITES
Explore these online sources with an adult:

Sound: The Science of Sound video | Science Trek | PBS

Sound Waves – General Science for Kids! video | Miacademy Learning Channel | YouTube

What Is Sound? for Kids video | Learn Bright | YouTube

Index

amplitude, 19
amplitude experiment, 16–19

conclusions, 6, 11, 15, 19, 23, 27
cone experiment, 28–29

decibels, 28
do-it-yourself experiment, 28–29

eardrum, 11
echoes, 27
energy, 8, 12, 15, 17, 19–20, 23
energy experiments, 8–11, 16–19

frequencies, 15, 23

glass harp, 23

hearing, 4–5, 11–12, 15, 18, 22, 24, 26–29
Hertz, Heinrich, 15
hertz (Hz), 15
hypotheses, 6–8, 11–12, 15, 17, 19, 21, 23–24, 27–28

mass, 23
molecules, 15–16, 19, 27

notes, 5, 21, 23

observations, 5–6, 8, 14, 16, 18–19, 22, 26, 29

pitch, 20, 23
pitch experiment, 20–23

questions, 5–6, 8, 16

scientific method, 6-7
scientists, 4–7, 11, 15, 28–29
solid objects experiment, 24–27
sonar equipment, 27
sound waves, 11, 15, 19, 24, 27–29
sound waves experiments, 8–15, 24–27

travel, 5, 7, 12, 15, 24, 27
travel experiment, 12–15

vibrations, 11–12, 15–16, 20–21, 23, 26–27
vibrations experiment, 20–23
vocal cords, 20

About the Author

Christine Taylor-Butler is an author with degrees in both civil engineering and art and design from the Massachusetts Institute of Technology (MIT). When she is not writing, she is reading, drawing, or looking for unusual new science ideas to write about. She is the author of more than 90 fiction and nonfiction books for children.